SAVING TASMANIAN DEVILS

rare earth

The publisher thanks Warwick Brennan and Jane McGee of the Tasmanian Department of Primary Industries, Parks, Water and Environment for their expert help in making this book.

First published in 2012
by **black dog books**,
an imprint of Walker Books Australia Pty Ltd
Locked Bag 22, Newtown
NSW 2042 Australia
www.walkerbooks.com.au

National Library of Australia Cataloguing-in-Publication entry:
Norman, Mark Douglas.
Saving Tasmanian devils / Mark Norman.
ISBN: 978 1 742031 80 4 (pbk.)
Series: Rare earth.
Subjects: Tasmanian devil – Habitat – Conservation – Australia.
Tasmanian devil – Pictorial works.
599.27

Typeset in Adobe Garamond Pro
Printed and bound in China

10 9 8 7 6 5 4

SAVING TASMANIAN DEVILS

Dr Mark Norman

black dog

rare earth

The noisiest marsupial

On the island of Tasmania, off the bottom of Australia, lives a tough little creature known as the Tasmanian devil. It is also known as the Tassie devil. It belongs to a group of **mammals** known as **marsupials**. This group includes kangaroos and koalas. Marsupials raise their young in a special pouch on their belly.

This cranky little animal needs our help.

Tasmanian devil

Kangaroo

Koala

Tasmanian devils might look cute but they get their name because they like to bite, fight and scream. They look cuddly but if you tried to pat one, you might lose a finger!

Only devils raised in captivity **trust humans enough not to bite them.**

Tasmanian devils use both sight and smell to track their food.

Tasmanian devils have excellent eyesight. They mainly see in black and white, but this vision works well at night. Devils are always sniffing the air for the smell of other animals, especially dead ones.

Tasmanian devils will eat almost any animal. They can catch and eat insects, frogs, lizards and birds, but what they seem to love most is dead animals.

When a large animal dies, gangs of devils can gather at the **carcass** for a feast. They are not very well behaved. There is lots of fighting and screaming as they compete for the best bits.

Tasmanian devils have very strong jaw muscles, and tough teeth that can even crunch through bones. They have a stronger biting pressure than lions and tigers.

Devils crush the bones of dead animals and swallow all the pieces. Some farmers like devils on their land as they completely clean up the bodies of cattle or sheep that have died.

Tasmanian devils live in a similar way to a group of dog-like animals called hyenas that live in Africa. Devils and hyenas are both scavengers, meaning they mainly eat dead animals.

Hyena

They both have similar-shaped heads with strong jaws – hyenas are also bone crackers. Both animals have longer front legs than back legs. The long front legs give them extra pull when they're tearing meat off dead animals.

Tasmanian devils have four babies at a time. For the first 100 days the joeys **are carried around in the mother's pouch.**

When the babies get bigger, the mother devil leaves the young at home, typically in a hollow log or burrow. For the next three months of the joeys' lives she goes out to find food and brings it back to them.

Once the young are about six months old they are strong enough to go out hunting with their mum. She will teach them how to find food and how to fight their way into gangs of feeding devils.

She also teaches them how to keep an eye out for predators such as wedge-tailed eagles. At about ten months old the youngsters set out to live on their own.

Wedge-tailed eagle

Striped skunk

If a devil is attacked, it can squirt a horrible-smelling liquid from under its tail – just like a skunk.

Tasmanian devils also have other tricks to help them stay alive. They can store fat in their tails. They live off their fat tails during hard winters when there is not much food around.

The nearest relatives of Tasmanian devils are spotted native cats known as quolls, and the now extinct Tasmanian tiger.

They all share a similar-shaped footprint where the toes are in a line at the front of the foot. Dog and cat footprints look more like a ring of flower petals.

Quoll

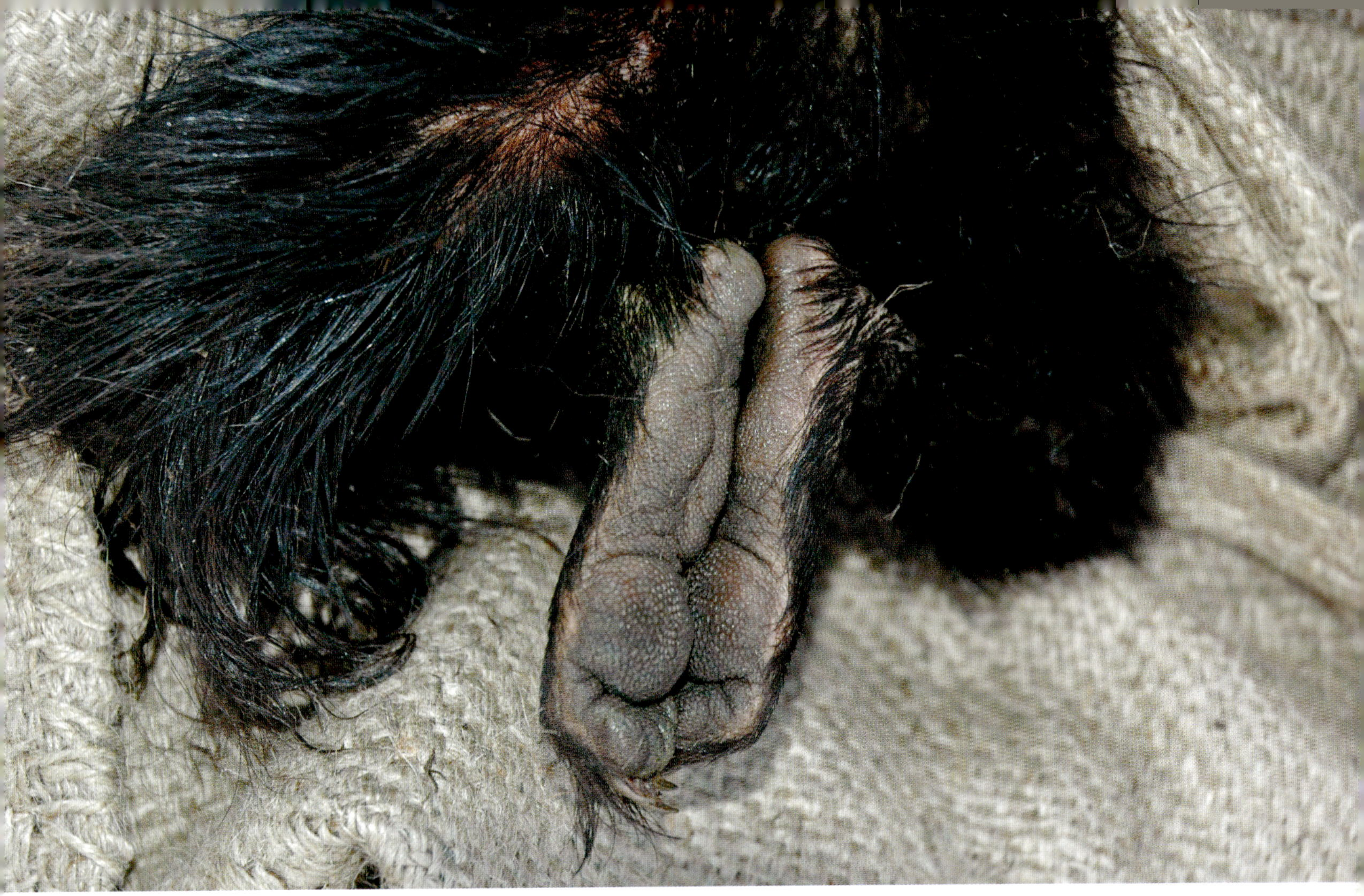

Tasmanian devil paw

Dog paw

Tasmanian tiger

Since 1996, wild Tasmanian devils have been suffering from a disease that causes growths on their faces and can eventually kill them. It is known as devil facial tumour disease.

This disease begins as small red growths around the mouth. As the growths get bigger, they can stop the devils from eating.

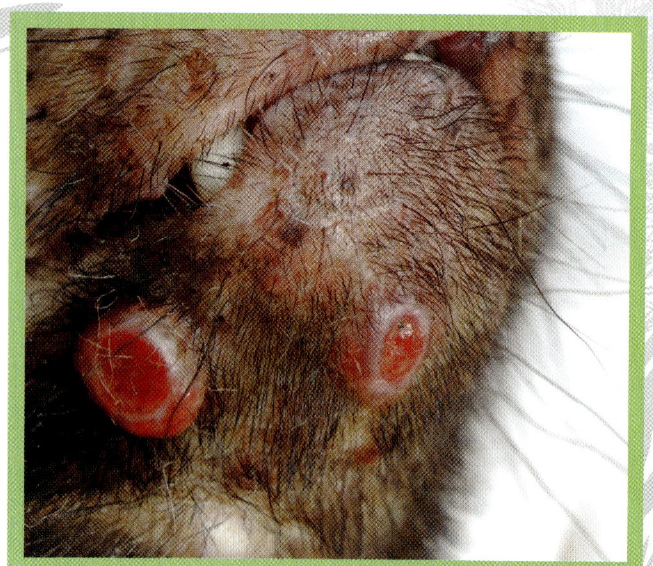

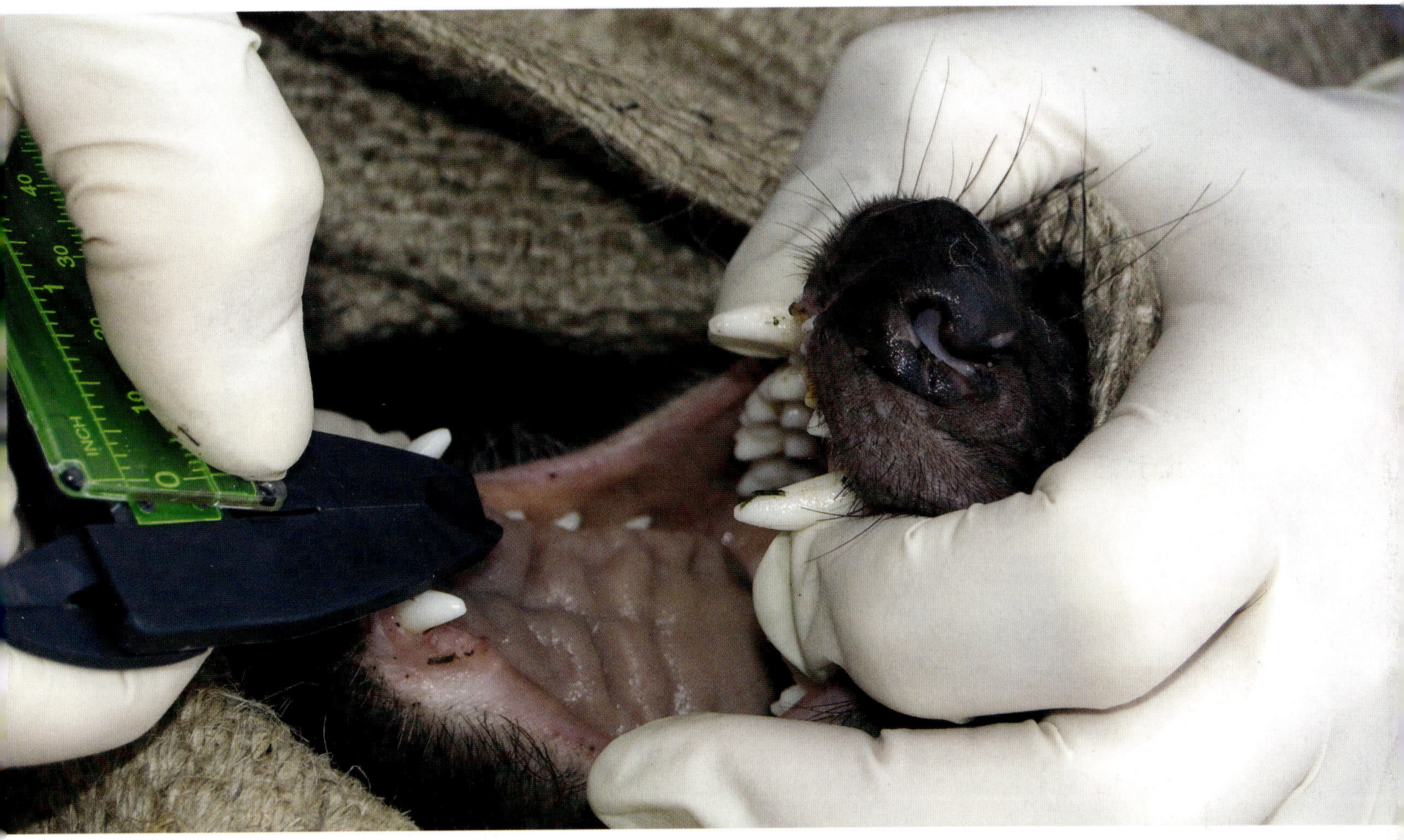

Scientists around the world are studying this disease to find ways to cure it. So far they have discovered that the devils catch the disease from other devils when they meet to eat at a dead animal. They are looking at what is special about the Tasmanian devils that do not catch the disease.

Many zoos and wildlife sanctuaries are raising populations of healthy devils. When a cure to the disease is found, these animals can be released back into the wilderness**.**

To help devils fight this disease, we need to keep healthy devils safe.

Devils often feed on animals killed by cars. This means they are on the road and can easily be killed by other cars. It is really important for drivers to slow down, especially at night.

You can help!

There are lots of things you can do to help Tasmanian devils.

Tell other people about how special devils are.

Find out if your nearest zoo is raising devils and how you or your school can help.

Help raise money for disease research.

Remind people that when they are driving at night, they should slow down and always look out for wildlife.

Write a letter to politicians and ask them to protect forests where the devil facial tumour disease has not reached, like the Tarkine National Park in northern Tasmania.

More facts about Tasmanian devils:

Tasmanian devils grow to the size of a small dog.

Tasmanian devils became extinct on the Australian mainland about 3000 years ago, maybe as dingos spread around Australia.

The Tasmanian devil is the largest living marsupial that eats meat. Bigger marsupials like kangaroos, koalas and wombats all eat plants.

Tasmanian devils can climb trees and swim rivers.

Tasmanian devil websites:

Save the Tasmanian Devil website:
www.tassiedevil.com.au

Tasmanian Parks and Wildlife service:
www.parks.tas.gov.au

Zoos Victoria captive breeding program:
www.zoo.org.au/tasmanian-devil

Glossary:

Joey: baby Tasmanian devil that lives in its mother's pouch.

Captivity: where humans keep animals in cages or reserves.

Carcass: the body of a dead animal.

Mammal: animals that raise their young on milk.

Marsupial: animals that carry their young in a pouch on their belly.

Wilderness: natural areas where there are no human activities.

Index: